AF405602

Operating Small Businesses

Geary Reid

Copyright © 2024 by Geary Reid

All rights reserved.

ISBN: 978-976-8305-95-4

Acknowledgments

Great thanks must be expressed to the following people:

The heavenly Father, for granting me the wisdom and inspiration to record the information in this book, which I began on May 10, 2022, and completed on May 16, 2022; my family, for their continued encouragement and support regarding various challenges; and several people who have assisted with reviewing and editing the book:

- Wonnetta Nicholson, Dipl. in Business Management and Administration
- Rev. Rickford Fanfair
- Pastor Jocelyn Dolphin
- Rendell F. Harry
- Joyce Sullivan

To you, the reader: have fun while reading, and grasp and practice what you learn so that this world will become a better place. Many people are depending on your guidance. We all need a shoulder to lean on and a hand to guide us.

Geary Reid

MBA, FCCA, FAAPM, MPM, CAT

Reid's Learning Institute and Business Consultancy

reidnlearn.com

Amazon: amazon.com/author/gearyreid

Facebook: Reid n Learn

Instagram: Reid n Learn

LinkedIn: Reid's Learning Institute
and Business Consultancy

199 Kuru - Kururu, Soesdyke Linden Highway
Guyana, South America

Table of Contents

Introduction

Operating small businesses can be challenging for many business owners. Operating a small business can be done from the owner's home, their garage, their parent's home, virtually, or in many other locations. However, as the business grows, some requirements must be met. Many small businesses started with just the owner, but as the business grew, it was necessary to employ other persons to assist in managing different operations of the business.

Gathering finances for small businesses can be a daunting task. Many times, owners struggle with the continuity of their small businesses because of a lack of finances. While relatives and friends might have been able to provide some finances, they were unable to generate the additional funds needed for the large-scale expansion of the business.

Effective communication is important for all businesses. It is not expected that business owners will spend their entire day making critical decisions, but they will be expecting employees in senior positions to make those critical decisions and provide them with updates. The feedback between business owners and employees will be a mixture of oral and written communication. With the implementation of Information Systems, such as Peach Tree, Quick Books, etc., business owners can have access to regular and accurate reports, which will help them in knowing what is happening with the business.

Small businesses must also comply with laws, regulations, policies, and procedures. There is a great need for compliance and better governance among small businesses. Policies and procedures are not intended to stymie progress but to enhance accountability.

Once people are employed in the business to assist the owners in managing the business and executing daily operations, then they will need some amount of training. The owners cannot perform all tasks by themselves since they may have another job and have decided to invest their resources into a small business with the intent of it becoming their main source of income, so they will have to delegate some authority to their employees.

Managing sales is critical for the business to generate revenue. Efforts must be made to continuously increase revenue. Promoting the business's goods and services is important to increase revenue. Establishing competitive selling prices help businesses to increase their competitiveness and increase their market share. If costs are not properly managed, then all the gains from an increase in revenue will be eroded.

An adequate amount of inventory must be acquired and maintained. Proper storage of inventory will prevent spoilage and ensure customers receive quality goods and services for the money they pay. Business owners, along with their managers, must seek to benefit from credit purchases from suppliers. It may mean that they will have to establish long-term contracts with suppliers, purchase large quantities, and make timely payments to suppliers to benefit from future credit purchases. Not all customers who approach the business for credit will be entitled to it. Managers must carefully manage the cash flow of the business to ensure its continuity.

1. Registering the business

Starting a small business requires the owner to follow some legal requirements. Within the first few weeks or months, when the business is started, some of the legal requirements may not be mandatory since the business owner is experimenting with the business. However, as the owners continue with the business, they are expected to manage the business professionally.

1.1 Owner

When the business is incorporated, the owners of the business will be identified since their names will be included on the business's registration form. In some small businesses, there may be one owner or several owners. Each owner must provide their full name and address when registering the business.

In some small businesses, one person may be the main person operating the business. For other small businesses, each owner may be providing equal support to the business as they utilize their different skills in finance, resources, and knowledge.

With large businesses, there may be executive or non-executive directors that manage the business. Once directors change, then such information must be submitted to the relevant authorities so that external records will be properly updated.

1.2 Business name

When a person or group of persons wants to open a business, they are expected to provide a name for the business. A business name provides a unique identification for the business. Sometimes, through the business name, people know what the business will be doing.

Let's use "Geary Reid Pharmacy" as an example. With the name mentioned, it is clear that the business was registered under the name of an individual. The name also indicates the type of the business, and in this case, it is a pharmaceutical business.

For another example, let's use "PJA hardware store." The name of this business is represented by three letters "PJA." Those letters stand for Patricia, John, and Ariel. Those three individuals are the owners of the business or represent the names of the owner's children or family members. The name also indicates the type of the business, and in this case, it is a hardware business.

Therefore, it may be easy to identify some types of businesses by looking at the business names. There are other businesses where the names are not adequate to identify the type of business.

1.3 Business plan

For the direction and success of the business, there is a need for a business plan. The business plan can be drafted by the owners, or they may request a professional to draft their business plan.

The business plan provides brief information about the future direction and operation of the business. Some aspects of the business plan will be adjusted as the business continues. However, it is important to have a starting point for owners and employees to work with.

For those business owners who may be seeking financing to start their business, they may need to present a business plan to the financial institution for consideration and approval. The business plan will be evaluated by representatives from the financial institution, and once it provides evidence that the business will be viable, then part or all of the finances will be provided. Sometimes, the business plan is created to attract investors, especially when the business needs additional financing or wants to expand.

The business plan will provide many of the business strategies and objectives. Some businesses will have separate documents to specify financial and strategic objectives if those objectives are not included in the business plan.

Table 1. Types of objectives

Types of objectives	Explanation
Financial objectives	Relates to the financial performance targets management has established for the organization to achieve
Strategic objectives	Relates to target outcomes that indicate a company is strengthening its market standing, competitive position, and future business prospects

(Extracted from Thompson et al., 2014)

Brief information on the marketing plan may be stated in the business plan. The business plan will address some aspects of Human Capital Management or people management.

A clear and reasoned strategy is management's prescription for doing business, its road map to competitive advantage, its game plan for pleasing customers, and its formula for improving performance (Thompson et al., 2014).

1.4 Mission statement

The Mintzberg theory describes a mission as "the organization's basic function in society, in terms of the products and services it produces for the clients" (ACCA P5 2010, 211).

Not all small business owners may start their business with a mission statement. Sometimes, as the business progresses, then a mission statement will be developed. However, other owners will ensure that they have a mission statement to work with from the inception. They know that the mission statement guides the future of the business, which stakeholders need to be informed of so that their energy and efforts will be put towards the same mission.

Table 2. Some characteristics of a mission statement

Characteristic	Explanation
Brevity	Easy to understand and remember
Flexibility	Can accommodate change
Distinctiveness	Makes the firm stand out
Open-ended	Not stated in quantifiable terms

(Extracted from ACCA P5, 2010)

Not all business owners know how to prepare a mission statement. However, they can pay for a professional or a firm to prepare their mission statement. The same firm that assists with the business plan could be used to prepare the mission statement.

The mission statement ought not to be complex. It must include some keywords or phrases that inform stakeholders of what they are expected to do and what they can expect the business to do for them.

Table 3. An expanded definition of the mission includes four elements

Elements of a mission	Details
Purpose	Why does the company exist? • To create wealth for shareholders? • To satisfy the needs of all stakeholders (e.g. employees, society at large)?
Strategy	A mission provides the commercial logic for the company, and so defines the following: • Nature of its business • Products/services offered; competitive position • The competence and competitive advantages by which it hopes to prosper, and its way of competing
Policies and standards of behavior	The mission needs to be converted into everyday performance. For example, a firm whose mission includes excellent customer service must pay attention to simple matters such as politeness to customers, the speed at which phone calls are answered, and so forth.
Values and culture	Values are the basic, perhaps unstated, beliefs of the people who work in the organization.

(Extracted from ACCA P5, 2010)

1.5 Business location

Some businesses may use a temporary location. At the time of registering the business, they may choose that location as the registered location of the business. Many businesses will change location as they continue to operate, but at the inception, when they are registering, they must provide a location.

Some owners may start their business by renting a property. After they have generated enough money and are established, then they may purchase their own building, and their location may also change.

Several small businesses, at the time of start-up, may be operating from the residence of one of the owners. Some owners start their businesses from their garages, their parents' property, etc. The owners knew that they had to start the business, and so they started the business. As the business grew, they were probably able to rent a property, and subsequently, they erected their own property.

Although some owners might have started on their property, the business grew, and they had to change location because they needed more land and larger property. With those changes, then the business location will be changed.

1.6 Business registration number

Business owners need to register their businesses. Once that is done, their businesses will become legal, and they can receive some benefits that are available to legal businesses. Also, registered businesses may have the advantage of competing for legal business, especially government and private sector contracts.

Most times, whenever governments have tenders, they will only accept submissions from registered businesses. Therefore, when owners establish their businesses, they must register their businesses as early as possible.

In most countries, there are designated agencies that are responsible for the registration of businesses. Most times, those agencies are government agencies. Those business owners who submit their documents will have to lodge their documents with the agencies for a few days, and once they meet all the requirements, then their business will be provided with a unique business registration number. With advanced technology, many business registrations can be done online. Those who need to register their businesses can download the form, insert their information, and then submit the form manually or electronically. There are also other options where the business can be registered online, as the applicants can insert all the information into a portal that is available to applicants. Whether the application process is done manually or electronically, business owners must ensure that their businesses are registered.

1.7 Tax identification number

If a business will not be producing taxable supplies, then the owners may not consider applying for Tax Identification Number (TIN). However, business owners should consider registering for TIN since there may be occasions when suppliers will provide them with taxable invoices, which will result in them having input VAT. Small businesses can grow. Therefore, business owners should prepare themselves from the beginning and ensure they register to charge Value Added Tax (VAT) to their customers.

1.8 Bank account and bank signatories

Many decades ago, business owners did most of their transactions in cash. However, times have changed, and many transactions are done through online payments or direct deposits to bank accounts. Therefore, there is less need for paper money. With that in mind, business owners must establish bank accounts.

At the establishment of the bank account, it may be just the business owners who sign all checks and bank payments. However, as the business progresses, then directors and managers may be allowed to sign off on bank payments.

For security reasons, business owners must keep most of their money in the bank. If customers want to engage in large payments, then the customers can be advised to make direct payments to the businesses' bank account, and once the customers provide proof that payment was made, then the goods and services will be provided to the customers.

At the initial stage, customers may make payments in local currency. However, as the business progresses, some customers may choose to make payments in foreign currencies. Some owners may have local and foreign bank accounts so that they will be able to accept local or foreign currency payments. Business owners may have to make foreign currency payments to suppliers. So there are many good reasons to establish both local and foreign currency bank accounts for businesses.

Most times, businesses will have at least two persons to sign off on any bank payment. Those bank signatories must provide certain documents to the bank before they are authorized to sign on behalf of the business. The business owners may have unlimited approval levels, whilst managers may have restricted signing limits for bank payments.

2. Gathering finance for the business

The requirements to access financing for small businesses can be a challenge for small business owners since the requirements may be more than some of them can adequately provide. The interest rates applied to small businesses are sometimes high, and small business owners find it difficult to borrow money to start their businesses. The owners of many small businesses are unable to expand their businesses because they are unable to gather adequate financing at a low interest rate and long payback duration.

[The interest] rate is the price paid (by the borrower) for the loan of money (made by the lender). (Lane P., 1966)

2.1 Factors to consider when borrowing

Any business owner who wants to borrow funds must evaluate the requirements needed to access the funds. Some of the requirements may be daunting. After business owners see some of the requirements, they may decide to grow their business slowly until they are in a position to provide the requisite requirements.

Borrowers . . . need money to finance their purchases. This includes businesses that need money to finance their investments or to expand their inventories as well as individuals who borrow money to purchase a new car or a new home. (Titman et al., 2016)

Figure 1. Factors to consider when borrowing

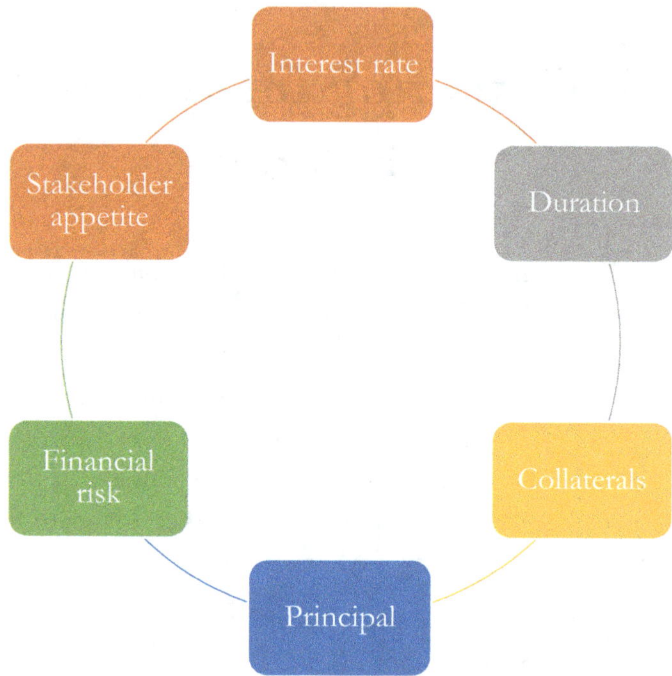

(All figures developed by the author unless otherwise noted.)

Although some business owners will agree to the interest rate from the financial institution, they may not be able to repay the amount within the short duration which was suggested by the financial institution. Smaller businesses are often provided with a short duration to repay borrowed funds because the financial institution may deem them as high risk.

2.2 Collaterals

Owners of small businesses may find it difficult to provide all of the collateral needed by some financial institutions. While some small businesses are registered, they may not be the owners of the properties they are using. Oftentimes, without documentation to prove ownership of some assets, financial institutions will not provide financing.

Figure 2. Collateral required by lending institutions

Transports and leases are not easily obtained by all small business owners. Some small business owners may be operating from their friends' and family's properties. They may start there and hope to gather financing so that they can expand their business and then later acquire land properly. The lack of ownership of small business owners continues to affect their planned expansions. While small business owners may reinvest their profits into the business, it will still take them a long time to grow their business. The lack of adequate financing for small businesses has caused many of them to close operations. However, business owners must constantly look for legal ways to obtain financing for their businesses.

3. Regular and effective communication

There must be vertical and horizontal communications within the business. Managers will give instructions to their subordinates, and managers have to receive instructions from the business owners. Suppliers will communicate with managers and other representatives of the business. Employees will have to communicate with customers. Communication never ceases in a business, even if the owners do not want to communicate.

Some businesses function even if the business owners are dormant. Employees may sometimes mention that they rarely see the owners. In some businesses, some employees never see the owners, but the businesses continue. When business owners put most systems in place, they do not have to be there to provide detailed instructions to all employees every day. Most owners will be delighted if their business can operate effectively without them saying much. Those owners will occasionally receive some reports of the business' performance, and they can evaluate the business based on the reports provided to them.

3.1 What is communication, and why is it necessary?

An individual may decide that they do not want to communicate, and they can lock themselves in a room and stay there without any communication device for the day. At the end of the day, they can achieve their target for the day by not communicating. However, for businesses, it is a different story. Even if businesses close for the weekend, communication still occurs. People may send emails to employees during the weekend. The security guards may have to report any situation at the business. The mechanics may service the vehicles on weekends when they are not in operation. Utility companies will submit utility bills even on the weekend. Maintenance personnel may be repairing the building during the weekend.

Communication is the process of creating, transmitting, and interpreting ideas, facts, opinions, and [feelings]. (Cole, 1993)

Communication will allow information and data to pass from one person to another person. The business owners will not be communicating every hour, but the information received from managers and other employees may keep them thinking for hours. A simple instruction from business owners often has the employees occupied for a long duration.

Communication does not always require decisions to be made. Information will flow from the sender to the receiver and from the receiver back to the sender.

Table 4. Communication process terms and explanations

Communication process term	Explanation
Source/Sender	The sender or source of communication is the person or organization with information to share with any person or group of people.
Encoding	This process involves putting thoughts, ideas, or information into a symbolic form.
Message	The encoding process leads to the development of a message that contains the information or meaning the source hopes to convey.

Channel	The channel is the method by which communication travels from one source or sender to the receiver.
Decoding	Decoding is the process of transforming the sender's message back into thought.
Receiver	The receiver is the person(s) with whom the sender shares thoughts or information.
Response	This is the receiver's set of reactions after seeing, hearing, or reading the message.
Feedback	Marketers are very interested in feedback, defined as part of the receiver's response that is communicated back to the sender.

(Extracted from Belch and Belch, 2015)

3.2 Effective communication leads to success

Effective communication between business owners and their employees will lead to success. Whenever business owners fail to be effective communicators, they will cause employees to speculate or make decisions that are not consistent with the success of the business. While owners do not have to be engaged in lengthy communication, they must be effective in their communication.

Figure 3. Communication can be effective or ineffective

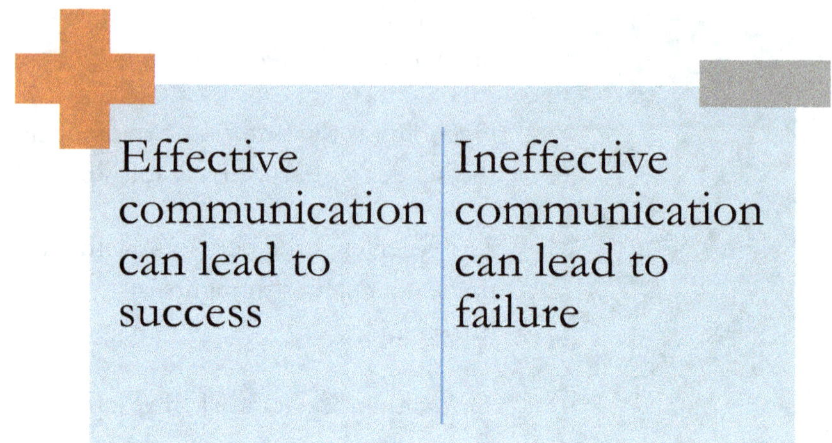

3.3 Written and oral communication

It may not be possible to write down everything that has to be communicated. Sometimes, when there is urgency, then oral communication will be the best option.

There must be written guidance within the business. For example, strategies, policies, and procedures are written communication. Written communication often takes a formal approach. When communication is in its written form, it provides consistency. Employees are often encouraged to reread the written documents so they understand what they have to do and what they are required to do.

When businesses employ people, those people will receive an employment contract in writing. Most of the details they need to know about their employment will be contained in their employment contract.

Table 5. Written and oral methods of communication

Method	Explanation
Written methods	These are principally letters, reports, notices, and printouts. By comparison with oral communication, the written word is more permanent and less liable to misinterpretation. It also encourages the sender of a message to think about it before dispatch. The disadvantages are that written communication takes longer to effect than oral methods and is still liable to misinterpretation, despite the efforts of the writer to be clear and logical.
Oral methods	These are usually meetings of one kind or another and telephone conversations. Oral communication may often lack the considered nature of written communication, but it does have the advantage of immediate feedback. In the case of face-to-face meetings, it has the added advantage of being reinforced by various forms of non-verbal behavior, such as facial expressions, gestures, and body posture. One of the major difficulties associated with oral communication is its transience – the spoken word is a sound and lasts only as long as it takes to pronounce it.

(Extract from Cole, 1993)

Besides written communication, there is always the need for oral communication. Many times, oral communication can reinforce written communication. There are times that once verbal agreements have been made, those agreements will have to be set down in written form.

When employees have problems, they often engage their managers in verbal communication. If the managers agree that the problem is severe, then the employee may be asked to put their oral communication into writing so that appropriate actions will be taken.

There will always be a need to address negative communication in the workplace. If negative communication is not addressed urgently, it will confuse people within the business, and instead of employees working as a team, they may be working against the success of the business.

4. Utilizing information systems

At the starting stage, some small businesses may operate a manual system of recording and processing their transactions. The manual system will require the employees to prepare handwritten receipts for funds received from customers. Financial transactions may be processed through a customized database that the business owners have experimented with. The database may only allow them to process summary information for financial transactions.

The manual system will not allow managers to see the real-time flow of all operations of the business. Manual recording of transactions may lack the details that may be needed for decision-making. For example, if summary data is processed, then managers will not be able to engage in drill-down reports. There may not be any data to assist with aging analysis for Accounts Receivable, Accounts Payable, and Inventory. Cash forecasting may be done by estimates rather than extracting data from an information system.

4.1 Investing in an information system

Business owners may agree with the managers to invest in an information system. They know that once they invest in an information system that they will capture details of most transactions. The ability to make faster and more critical decisions will be aided by the reports they can extract from the information system.

Figure 4. The shifting trend in people's dependency on information flow

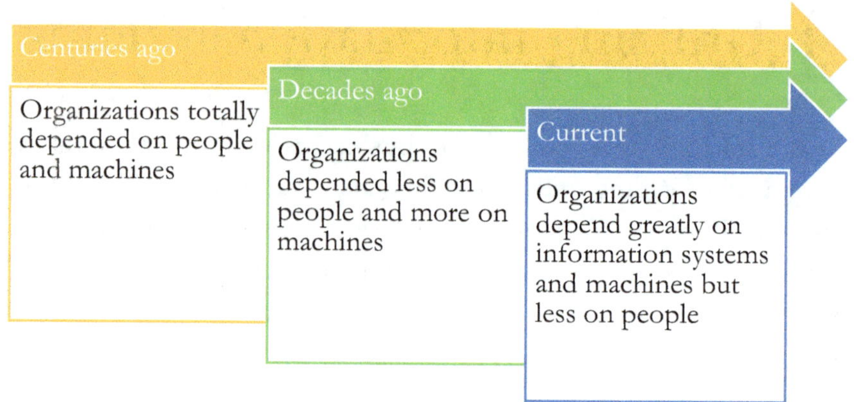

Acquiring an information system must be seen as an important investment for the business. Those who are responsible for designing the technical specifications for the information system must ensure that the information system can generate most of the reports they need for decision-making. They must also ensure that the information system can process all operations and financial transactions quickly and that the database is updated immediately.

"Management information systems (MIS) can be distinguished from other information systems within an organization by reference to the specific features of that system" (ACCA 3.4, 2003):

- Provision of support for structured decision-making at all management levels

- Provision of online access to the transaction processing system (TPS) of the organization to give summary information on the performance of the organization

- An internal rather than external focus, with detail being provided on the organization itself rather than the competitors of the overall economic environment

- Provision of more detailed information on the organization's operations where required. This is the drill-down facility so often associated with MIS.

- Use of relatively simple programs to produce summaries and comparisons rather than more detailed information models or statistical techniques found in a DSS

4.2 Integrated information systems

As the business progresses, the business owners may choose to have an integrated information system. With the integrated information system, they can capture data from most of the departments. If the business was using a basic information system, then they may want to acquire an integrated information system that generates more reports for them. However, before switching from an information system to an integrated system, management can consider doing parallel runs. They can also consider phased conversion. The intention is to ensure that the information from both systems is accurate before fully agreeing to use the integrated information system alone.

Table 6. Approaches to using the new software

Approaches	Explanation
Parallel running	This involves running the new system in parallel with the old system and making a comparison of the results of both. If the new system performs the same as the old system as far as control details are concerned, then the go-ahead can be given for the live running.
Direct conversion	This involves the direct conversion from the old to the new system without any parallel running. Direct conversion is often the only practical approach to conversion, although there is the danger that the new system will not work correctly and that the organization will be in serious trouble. The method of control must be established.

Phased conversion	A complete section of the existing system is run on the new system. The section chosen needs to be complete. If that part is successfully run, then other parts of the existing system will be transferred over to be run on the new system until eventually, the whole of the system has been changed over.
Pilot operation	Here, the conversion is carried out department by department or branch by branch. Thus, if a manual sales ledger is being converted, it might be carried out geographically area by area. Each area would be run in parallel until satisfactory. Then the manual system is dropped, and the next area runs in parallel.

(Extracted from ACCA 2.1, 2001)

The integrated information system will contain several modules. Those modules will interconnect with other modules. Because some modules are interconnected, it makes it easy for managers within the various departments to see activities that have occurred in other departments. The integrated information system allows the business to operate as one rather than operating in silos.

Those managers who have access to generate reports will be able to assess many aspects of the business. If managers want to generate a full report of the business, then they can do so any time of the day since information is processed in real-time, immediately after employees process their transactions. The full report, when generated, will allow them to have an operational and financial overview of the business. Many business owners have invested in integrated information systems so they have access to more reports. The integrated information system also gives managers more information to carefully evaluate the business without having to rely on junior employees for important details.

Figure 5. Business modules and sections in an integrated information system

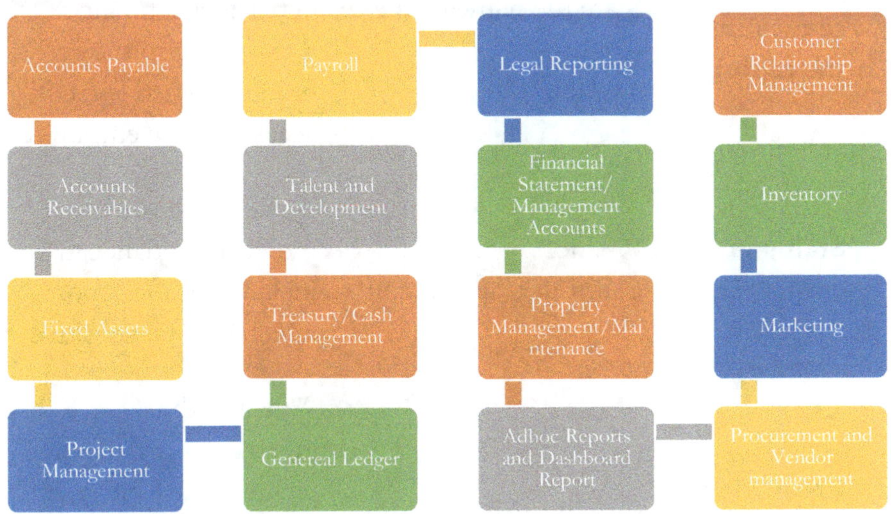

4.3 Dashboard reports

Business owners sometimes need to extract summary reports from the integrated information system. When many department heads generate manual reports, those reports may not always be consistent.

Many integrated information systems have their own built-in dashboard report. However, some businesses may have to design their own dashboard reports. They must determine what features are needed from a dashboard report before it is so designed.

Table 7. Features for the dashboard report development

What is needed	Example	Comments/reasons for the details
Name of department	Finance	This report will only be made available to a finance employee

The person requesting the report	State the name of the person	Information system and technology department/finance department to the predetermined level of access for the employee
Status of employee	Finance controller/accountant	Based on access level, then certain data can be included in the report, which may be sensitive
Frequency of report	Once weekly	Will alert the information system and technology department how often the employee may need to generate this report
Software module for the extraction of the data	General ledger	State the module that the report can extract the relevant data since the information system and technology department may not be aware of the certain module as some details in the general ledger may not be available to other modules
The format for output reporting	Microsoft Word, Excel, PDF	When the report is built, it will be

		produced in the format identified by the user
Size of paper to print on	8 ½" x 11" or 11" x 14"	The user may want to print the report, so the choice of paper will be important
Name of the report	Weekly cash balances comparison	When the name has been identified, the information system and technology department will build the report using the same name
Period range	1st of the month to 7th of the month or any other 7-day period	Choose any seven days or any other appropriate period

Once they agree to the features that their dashboard report must possess, then they will have their experts build those templates in the integrated information system. The dashboard reports must allow managers and owners to make quick and accurate decisions about the business. Dashboard reports allow the users of the system to analyze the performance of the business with little input from other employees.

5. Embracing policies and procedures

There is always the need to develop policies and procedures for new businesses. Oftentimes, when small businesses start, the owners operate from their understanding of business. However, within certain industries, there are standard practices that they must adhere to. As small businesses continue their operations, their owners and managers must provide the employees with the specific practices they must follow. If an established business continues to operate without policies and procedures, there will be chaos and confusion, and it will be difficult for auditors to evaluate its performance.

5.1 Should businesses embrace policies and procedures?

When a business is starting up, the owners and managers often may not see any need for policies and procedures. However, if the owners and managers do not want to establish policies and procedures, they may be forced to implement them, as they have to standardize the way the business operates. Both policies and procedures can be designed for almost all aspects of the business. Policies and procedures must not restrict the growth of the business but allow the business to be successful as it operates. A business should aim to provide exceptional quality products and professional services and not merely act as competition to another.

Figure 6. Why should businesses embrace policies and procedures?

5.1.1 Regulatory requirements

Within some business sectors, there are regulatory requirements. Those regulatory requirements may be supported by policies and procedures.

When governments establish Value Added Tax (VAT), it may force some businesses to develop policies and procedures that govern how they account for sales and purchases since they both affect the correct computation of input and output VAT. If the revenue agency recognizes that some businesses are not recording the VAT transactions, then those businesses will be penalized.

Most governments have acts and laws that govern the labor force. Therefore, business owners and managers will have to develop human resources policies and procedures to support the labor acts and laws.

5.1.2 Allowing businesses to achieve their objectives and strategies

With the establishment of policies and procedures, most business owners review the actual performance against the objectives and strategies that were established. When there are policies and procedures in the business, employees will have to follow formal ways of operating. Therefore, the actions of the employees can be traced and measured.

5.1.3 Consistent operation

The establishment and enforcement of policies and procedures are to ensure that there is a consistent operation in the business. If there is a regular change of employees within the business, they can produce inconsistent results. However, when there are policies and procedures in place that both new and old employees follow, then the outcome will be consistent.

5.1.4 A tool to evaluate employees' performance

Employees' performance must be evaluated. Without policies and procedures, it is difficult to evaluate their performance since there is hardly anything to measure them against. When there are policies and procedures, an employee's performance can be evaluated in a step-by-step approach against those guidelines.

5.1.5 A guide for auditors to evaluate the business

Auditors often will review an operation and transaction against any written documentation the business has agreed to use. The policies and procedures provide written documentation that the auditor will use to evaluate the business. A written policy and procedure are always better than the best-experienced employee's memory.

5.1.6 Safeguarding owner's assets and liabilities

Most times, owners will leave their assets and liabilities in the hands of the managers and other employees of the business. While the owners may not be there to approve and review every detail of their business, they can recruit the service of an auditor to evaluate the managers and other employees to determine who did the correct things.

For example, some businesses have policies that guide managers concerning seeking finances for the business. The policy may guide in terms of what percentage or amount managers can borrow for the business. For example, the policy that governs borrowing may specify that managers can borrow up to 35% of the business's total assets. Another policy may stipulate that the maximum credit approved to a customer must not exceed a specified amount. These safeguards are important to help managers to operate within the level of authority entrusted to them.

5.2 Implementing policies and procedures

Once policies and procedures are established, then they must be implemented. It will take time to write policies and procedures, and the business owners must then ensure that those policies and procedures become operational.

Before some policies and procedures are implemented, there will be a need for training. The training will be to ensure that employees know what is required of them and the way those tasks and or responsibilities are to be carried out. In the absence of training, employees may only implement some of the policies and procedures, and that will defeat the whole purpose.

5.3 Reviewing policies and procedures

After policies and procedures are established and implemented, then it is important to review them. Some policies and procedures will require modification.

If some aspects of the business change, then it will be important to review the policies and procedures that govern those operations. If it is discovered that all things are working in accordance with the existing policies and procedures, then no changes will be necessary.

However, if some aspects of the operation change, then modifications to certain policies and procedures will be required.

6. Recruiting employees

Many times, small business owners start off doing most of the work themselves, but as the businesses grow, there will be a need to recruit people to meet the demands of those businesses. The skills and knowledge some business owners possess may be limited and cannot be used to grow the business beyond where it started. However, some business owners are willing to recruit people who are professional and experienced to realize the growth of the business.

Some business owners are afraid to give other people the opportunity to manage the day-to-day operation of the business for them. If the owners trust others, then they may get more done through those employees whom they recruited to manage different aspects of the business. Trust is essential in business.

Human resource recruitment is a practice or activity carried on by an organization with the primary purpose of identifying and attracting potential employees (Hughes, Ginnett, and Curphy 2015).

6.1 Where to find suitable applicants?

When owners have to recruit people to fill various positions, they have to look at their available options. Within small businesses, there will be a limited pool of skilled and qualified people to fill some vacancies. With small businesses, there may not be enough employees to take up senior positions. Therefore, there may be the need to seek external people to fill some vacancies. If the owners want to make changes to the current culture within the business, they may prefer to recruit external people who may bring their own culture to their business. However, their culture should not be counter-productive or contrary to the owner/s goal, policies, beliefs, and convictions.

Figure 7. Sources to recruit people

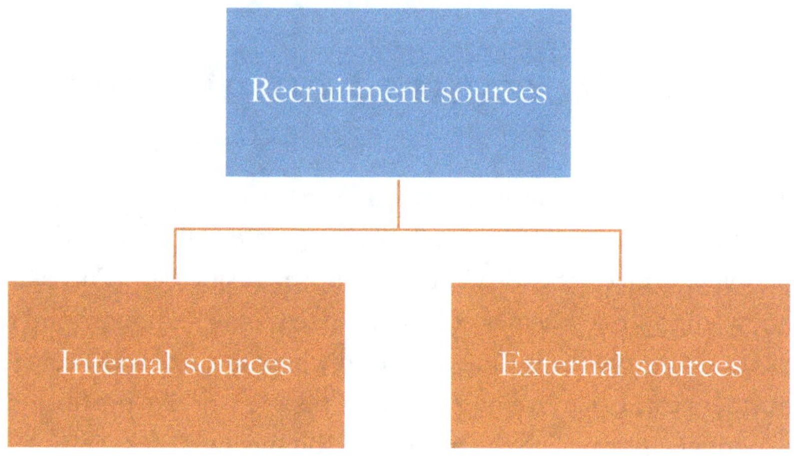

(Developed from Noe et al., 2015)

6.2 Setting up an interview panel

Business owners sometimes know that they need people to fill some vacancies. They may advertise those vacancies, but fail to establish an interview panel, since the owner may think he or she is competent enough to interview all applicants. When establishing an interview panel, these are some important questions for consideration:

- Does the individual possess any interviewing skills?

- Does the individual have technical knowledge in any similar area?

- Does the individual have practical experience in that area?

- Is the individual independent in their judgment?

- Is the individual working toward the success of the organization?

- Does the individual have any grievances with the organization?

- Is the individual working toward political ambition or personal gains?

Some business owners may want their friends and families to be part of the interview panel. However, the questions above will identify suitable panelists and will eliminate unsuitable people from the interview panel.

6.3 Background checks of applicants

While some candidates may do well in the interview, it is important to conduct background checks on successful applicants. The background checks can be done by the owner, an authorized employee of the business, or an independent recruitment firm.

The background checks will provide important information about the candidates. The owners must be satisfied that they are recruiting candidates who possess a good reputation in their societies and the information they provided during the interview is accurate.

Selected candidates may have to present a police clearance. That document is important for employers to know if the candidate had any previous criminal records that may rule them out as being a quality candidate for employment. It must also be noted that a past criminal record should not always be used to rule out an applicant for a position since the applicant could have since reformed.

7. Training employees

When candidates are recruited, they may need some amount of training. Managers and business owners must invest in developing their employees' knowledge and skills base. The training session may be a refresher session for some employees, but it may be useful to reinforce some important things that they ought or ought not to be doing.

Training is a planned effort to facilitate the learning of job-related knowledge, skills, and behavior by employees. (Noe et al., 2015)

Too many organizations fail to invest in their employees. Lack of training of employees has resulted in some businesses not being successful enough. Training must be provided to existing employees and recruits so they all have the same knowledge to make the business successful.

Figure 8. Training to be provided to existing and new employees

7.1 Establish a training plan

Training often equips employees to increase their performance, which will, in turn, improve the performance of the business. However, if the owners are desirous of great results from their training, then they must establish a training plan.

The training plan must be established to suit the needs of the business. The owners and managers must spend some time planning what things need to be addressed during the training.

Most times, if a business has peak periods where employees are very busy, then training can be provided during off-peak periods. When planning training sessions, the owners have to decide if they are willing to lose a few hours of sales so that front-line employees will be trained or if the owners will be paying overtime to employees who will be trained on weekends and holidays.

Figure 9. A training plan will include

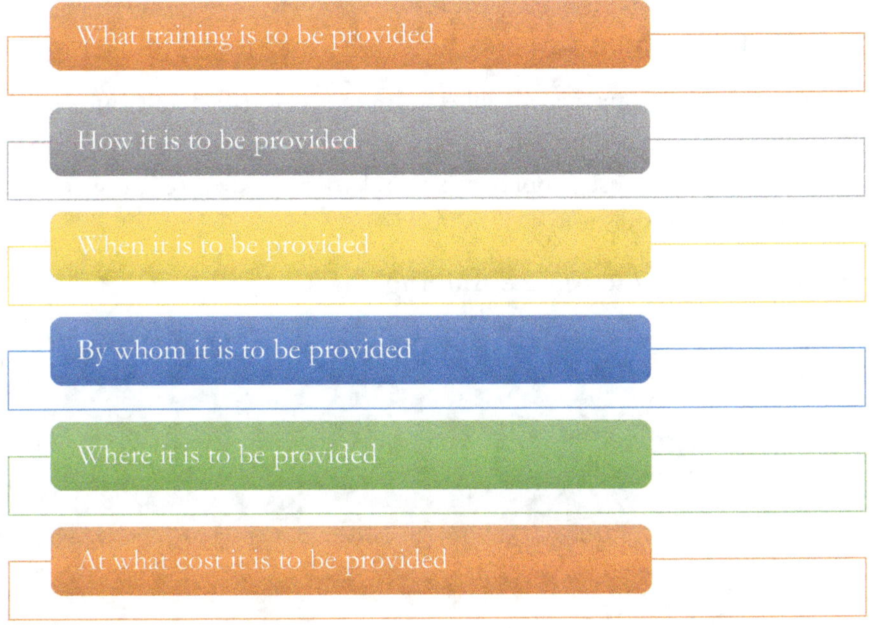

(Extract from Cole, 1993)

During training, snacks or lunch may have to be provided. A budget must be established for training. In the annual budget, some funds must be set aside for training.

Training can be scheduled for junior employees and senior employees at different intervals. Different facilitators may be needed for training different levels of employees, as the level of comprehension will be different between the junior and senior employees.

Identifying the location for the training is another important thing for management to take into consideration. For some employees, when training is conducted away from their offices and workstations, they tend to be more dedicated to the training.

When deciding on training, management must also decide if training will be done in a classroom setting or if persons may be trained at their desks. Trainees ought to be encouraged to take notes while the training is being conducted.

7.2 Reducing training costs

Business owners must not make training a one-off event but seek to provide regular training once the need exists. Regular training can be costly to the business. There are several ways to keep training costs as minimal as possible.

Figure 10. Ways to reduce training costs

Train many employees at once

Document processes or procedures of how tasks are to be completed

Establish manuals for tasks

Engage each person within each department to train at least one person in that department

Job rotation

Upload recent training video, manual, etc. on intranet, website, social media

Recruit highly skilled and experienced staff who are within the same industry or have operated in the same position

If the business has a high staff turnover, then regular training may be needed. Therefore, the owners need to be deliberate in order to keep training costs low while, at the same time, achieving the desired outcome.

Some owners may see training costs as very expensive, but they should reconsider training as an investment towards the employees and a benefit for the business. With the training provided, many employees can reduce the costs some businesses incur by improving their performance and also increasing sales.

Both new and existing businesses must invest in training their employees. The knowledge and experience gained by employees from the training may cause them to have the desire to stay longer with the business because they understand more about the business and see themselves as important within it.

7.3 Identifying training needs

Training needs can be identified at different levels. Business owners and managers must be alert to identify many of the training needs. After identifying training needs, then they must prepare the training plan so that they will budget accordingly.

Figure 11. Identifying training needs at different levels

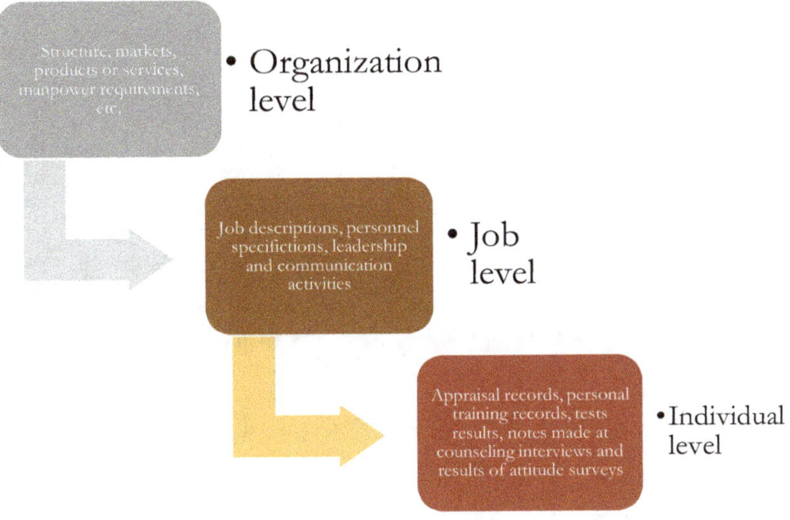

(Developed from Cole, 1993, p. 317)

Training needs can be identified by internal and external sources. The combination of information from inside and outside ought to help management carefully plan how they will address those training needs. With increased competition, business owners must ensure that their employees are properly trained so that they will constantly deliver quality output and services.

8. Delegating to employees

One of the challenges many owners face is that once they start up the business they feel that they must always be involved in every detail of its running. They are afraid to let anyone assist them with the business. Being afraid or over-cautious can be directly related to trust issues with people.

If business owners want their businesses to grow, they have to learn to delegate. Sometimes, their knowledge may be limited, and once they allow managers and other employees to manage the business, they can see more being done.

8.1 What is delegation, and what is its importance?

While many owners want to do many things in their businesses, they cannot do everything by themselves. As the business expands, owners will have to concentrate more on strategic matters rather than operational matters.

Delegation is the process by which an individual manager or supervisor transfers part of his legitimate authority to a subordinate but without passing on the ultimate responsibility which has been entrusted to him by his supervisor. (Cole, 1993)

When managers and owners delegate, they free up themselves to utilize some time and activities as they desire. They then allow other persons to execute those delegated activities and, oftentimes, they will review the activities.

Delegation is a relatively simple way for leaders to free themselves of time-consuming chores, give followers developmental opportunities . . . and [increase] the number of tasks accomplished by the workgroup, team or committee. Delegation implies that someone has been empowered by a leader, boss, or coach to take responsibility for completing certain tasks or engaging in certain activities. (Hughes et al., 2015)

As owners delegate more activities to managers and other employees, the business will have more people who can complete the same activities. That is always welcome news, as the same activities will be executed by different people, and sometimes, those who learn to execute those activities may be more efficient in their delivery.

Figure 12. Why delegating is important

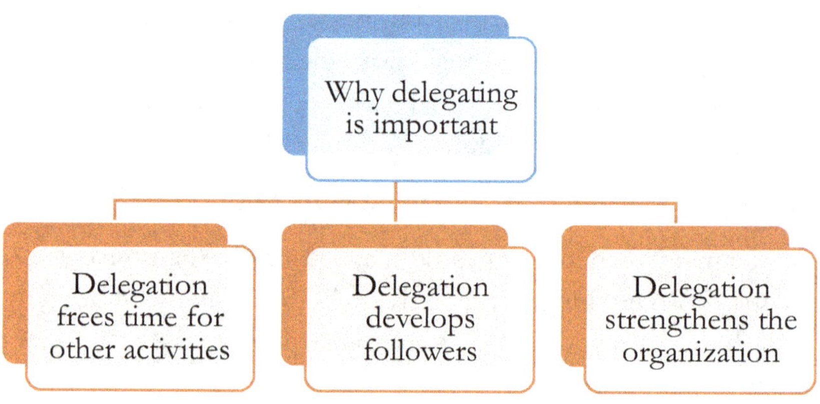

(Extracted from Hughes et al., 2015)

8.1.1 Delegation frees time for other activities

Many owners may feel that because they started the business, then they must continue to manage every detail of the business. However, those leaders must learn the importance of delegation. Although delegating responsibilities, some owners micromanage their businesses and lose production because staff are not allowed the scope to be themselves in delivering the quality service required.

A business might have started with just a few customers but later increased to hundreds and thousands of customers. With those increases, owners must shift their focus and allow more people to perform some activities in the business as they spend more time on long-term planning.

8.1.2 Delegation develops followers

Sometimes, when managers and business owners delegate, they allow their followers to develop. Many times, subordinates will like to do some of the things they see the managers and supervisors doing. So they anxiously await the opportunity for some authority to delegate some activities to them.

When more people are able to do the same things, it allows more things to be completed in less time. Followers are oftentimes motivated when they can execute some activities and receive positive feedback from their leaders of a good job done by them.

8.1.3 Delegation strengthens the organization

The business is strengthened when several employees can perform the same activities. When business owners delegate authority to some employees, they can go on vacation, and the business will continue to function as though they were there.

If business owners have to travel overseas, they must be confident that their business will continue to function without interruption. The business will be stronger when many employees can do the same activities; thus, managers and owners do not have to micromanage each employee. The time taken to micromanage employees can be utilized to help the business to grow.

8.2 Make delegation effective

Business owners and managers must make delegation effective. They must plan what they want to do. The planned activities must be assigned to competent employees to whom they will delegate some authority. Not all employees in the business will be prime candidates for activities to be delegated to them. Therefore, when suitably qualified employees are identified, then they must be allowed to grow within the business.

The first step leaders should take when deciding [on] what to delegate is to identify all their present activities. This should include those functions regularly performed and decisions regularly made. (Hughes et al., 2015)

Identifying what has to be delegated important for managers and business owners. When authority is delegated, and the employees perform the activity efficiently, then managers and owners must compliment the employee for accepting the authority and properly executing the activity. Many times, employees will complain that they have completed the activities delegated to them but they have not received feedback on their performance.

Figure 14. Principles of effective delegation

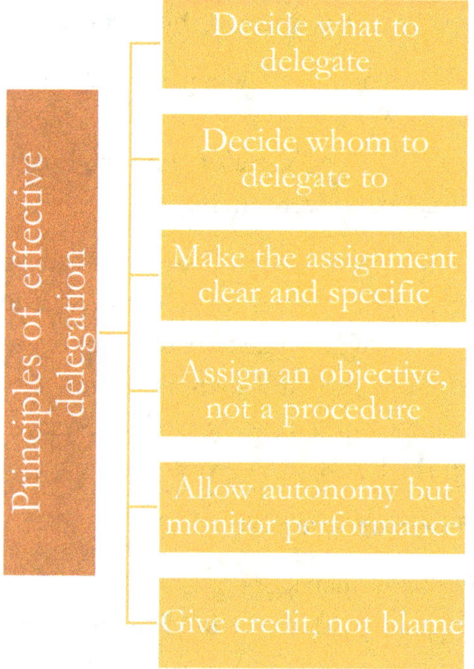

(Extracted from Hughes et al., 2015)

When authority is delegated to subordinates, managers and owners must allow that individual to function with some autonomy. The manager and owner can then monitor their performance of the activities. Each individual will have their own approach to performing a given activity. However, their outcomes are expected to be the same or similar. When employees know that they will be given autonomy to perform their duties, then they will operate with independence and may be creative with what they have to do. Owners are sometimes surprised to see the results from those employees whom they have delegated authority to.

9. Vacations for employees

Owners and managers sometimes become sick because they operate like robots, believing that they must be at work every day. While there are many things to be done, employers must learn to rest.

With small businesses, many times, the owners think that they cannot leave the business even for one day. They believe that if they are not there, then their businesses will crumble. However, if they think that the business will crumble in a single day, then it means that they have not recruited the right set of people or they have not trained employees well. If employees are properly trained and given opportunities to perform their duties professionally, then leaders and owners can go on vacation, and their business will continue in their absence.

9.1 Designing a vacation policy

Just because a business is small doesn't mean that it must operate in an unprofessional manner. Small businesses must have policies and procedures. Included in their human capital policy must be a policy or procedure on vacations.

Junior and senior employees need to rest their bodies. When owners arrange for the design of a vacation policy, they must include the views of the employees or seek guidance from experienced persons in the same sector. For some business sectors, it may be a standard practice to offer different levels of vacation time for employees, since their work demands are different.

Table 8. Vacation varies because of many factors

Conditions affecting vacation	Example
Length of time that the individual has worked for the organization	Employees with a few years may be entitled to two weeks, four weeks, and more.
The employee's status	The vacation may differ based upon the employee's status; for example, junior staff may be entitled to two weeks, managers, four weeks, and executives, more than four weeks.
Conditions in which the employee has to work	Factory workers and those that work under physically challenging conditions may be entitled to more vacation than office employees. Persons who are exposed to chemicals, paints, coal mines, etc. may receive more vacation than those in the office.
Full-time or part-time employee	Full-time employees will receive vacation according to their employment contract. Part-time employee's vacation will be subject to many factors, for example, the number of days worked in the period, the employee's status in the organization's hierarchy, etc.

Employees must be compensated for their vacations. While some owners and managers may feel that the organization is losing money when employees are on vacation, they must treat employees as important assets to the business.

Even machines need rest. The design of the vacation policy and procedure must allow employees to have enough rest so that they will return to work rejuvenated. When employees are properly rested, they will be more productive than if they were tired.

Figure 15. Benefits of rested employees

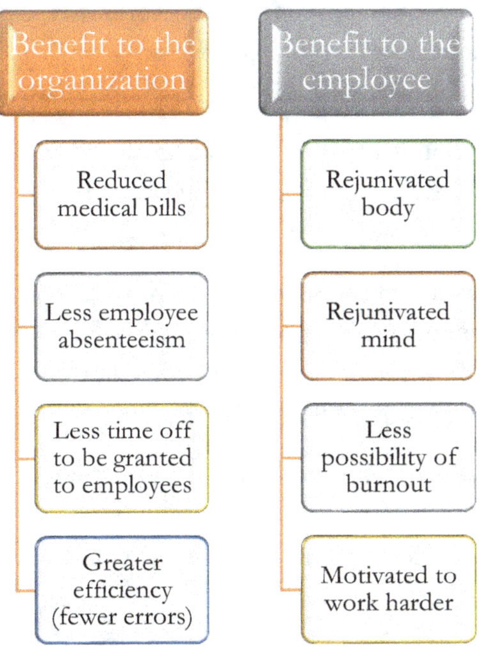

9.2 Sickness and maternity leave

There must be clear guidance for employees to follow concerning sickness and maternity leave. Employees often get sick without any warning signs. While employees are sick or on maternity leave, the business is expected to still compensate them since they are still employed by the organization. However, they must be guided in terms of how much must be paid once they are on sick and maternity leave.

In some businesses, employees will be paid for the early part of their sick leave. A similar thing happens when employees are on maternity leave. However, after the specified days have elapsed, then employees who are on sick and maternity leave will be paid a specific amount or a specific percentage of their remuneration. The remaining part of their benefits will have to be claimed from insurance, medical, and social security institutions.

9.3 When is an employee entitled to a vacation?

Employees who recently joined the business may not be entitled to a vacation. They may have to work for several months or at least complete one year of continuous work.

If, by chance, a recent employee wants to use vacation time for an emergency, then their annual vacation will be prorated. In some businesses, recently joined employees may be offered no leave if they did not complete their first year of work.

Whatever policies are in place for employees' vacations, they must be known to all employees. If possible, employees must be provided with a copy of the business's vacation policy. For some businesses, vacation information will be placed on the business's intranet.

In some businesses, employees' vacations may be progressive as they work more years with the organization. Therefore, an employee who recently joined the organization will not be entitled to the same length of vacation as an employee who has worked many years with the business.

Sometimes, employees may not want to take their vacation for various reasons. There are other times when employers may not want to approve employee vacations because they have a great need for those employees. However, employees should be allowed to utilize some, if not all, of their vacation leave during the year. There are risks associated when employees do not utilize their vacation. Both the employee and employer will be affected by those risks.

Figure 16. The risks of delaying a vacation

Risk to the employee

- Demotivated
- Takes longer to perform basic tasks
- Lost family and relationships becasue too much time is spent with the organization

Risk to the employer

- Employee can become sick and unable to work for a short or long period
- Employee may begin to make many errors, which can be costly to the organization
- Employee may collude with others to perform harmful acts againts the employer (stealing, etc.)

In a small business, there may not be many employees, and therefore, when one employee goes on vacation, it affects some aspects of the business. While business owners may want to keep employees at work despite the employees being due for a vacation, those business owners must put other systems in place for other employees to fill any temporary void. Sometimes, business owners can employ temporary workers when permanent employees go on vacation. The work must continue, and employees must utilize the vacation that they have earned.

10. Managing sales

People often become involved in business because they have something tangible or intangible to sell. For instance, customers will go to markets and purchase vegetables and fruits to prepare healthy meals. The vegetables are tangible, and after customers pay for the products, they can take those products to their homes.

However, some businesses have intangible services to sell to customers. For example, a person who needs a body massage will visit a beauty spa for a massage. Someone who needs to start a business may seek the service of a consultant. Based on the advice of the consultant, they may start their business. Both the consultancy service and the massage are services. Despite the customer paying for the service, the customers cannot feel or see the service they paid for. Services have some unique characteristics, as shown in the table.

Table 9. Characteristics of service

Characteristics of service	Explanation
Intangibility	Lack of substance (has no physical form)
Inseparability (simultaneity)	Created at the same time it is consumed
Variability (heterogeneity)	Output for each service varies (not the same, but similar)
Perishability	Services are innately perishable

No transfer of ownership	Services do not result in the transfer of property

(Extract from ACCA P5, 2010)

Whether a business has goods or a service, they have something to sell to the public. If they want their business to continue, then the business owner must manage sales to generate enough revenue.

10.1 Designing a sales strategy

Managers, along with owners, must design their sales strategy. This will provide them with guidance on what they plan to do for the next year, two years, or five years. Without a sales strategy, the sales team will be selling their products and services but will not have any target that they are working towards. The sales strategy must be designed before the fiscal year begins.

10.2 Establishing a sales budget

The sales strategy must be converted to sales numbers for the sales team to work with. Oftentimes, a sales budget is produced to support the sales strategy. The sales budget can be broken down into sales by product and sales by period.

A budget is a plan expressed in financial and/or quantitative terms for a specified period . . . in the future. (ACCA 2.4, 2001)

Table 10. PJA sales by quarters and products

Calendar month	Quarter	Product A ($)	Product B ($)
January	Quarter 1	17,800	8,750
February	Quarter 1	19,200	9,350

March	Quarter 1	20,000	7,900
	Subtotal per quarter	57,000	26,000
April	Quarter 2	22,000	11,300
May	Quarter 2	24,000	9,700
June	Quarter 2	25,000	7,000
	Subtotal per quarter	71,000	28,000
July	Quarter 3	23,500	4,500
August	Quarter 3	27,500	6,500
September	Quarter 3	30,500	8,000
	Subtotal per quarter	58,000	19,000
October	Quarter 4	42,000	3,300

November	Quarter 4	54,000	4,100
December	Quarter 4	68,000	2,600
	Subtotal per quarter	164,000	10,000
	Grand total	322,500	72,000

In Table 10, PJA plans to generate $322,500 from the sales of Product A. The sales for Product A and Product B are broken down into quarters. With Product B, PJA budgeted to generate revenue of $72,000 for the entire year.

The sales budget must be presented to the sales team. In some businesses, the sales team may be critically involved in preparing the sales budget for the owners to approve. That is taking a bottom-up approach toward management. PJA's sales budget provides monthly sales. If the sales team is unable to meet the sales for a particular month, then they will have to increase their sales for the new month until they meet or surpass their sales budget for that quarter. With detailed sales information, managers and their support employees must help the business to meet its sales target.

10.3 Develop a sales team

Many businesses which are involved in selling goods and services will have a sales team. However, for recently established small businesses, they will have to develop their sales team.

The sales team, once developed, must be informed of the sales strategy and sales budget. There must be constant communication between the sales team and the owner about how the target will be met within the fiscal year.

10.4 Motivating the sales team

Efforts must be made to motivate the sales team. There are times that the sales team can become demotivated, especially when they have a huge budget to accomplish. When competitors are offering the same product and service, then the sales team will have to work harder.

During weekly, monthly, or quarterly meetings, the sales team must be reminded of their target. They must be informed of their accomplishment for any given period, so they will know what they need to do or what they ought not to do. Some small businesses may manage sales by using manual reports. Large businesses may have an integrated information system with a sales module. Through the sales module, the sales team will be able to evaluate their daily, weekly, and monthly performance, and see any by-products. Once the owners see the sales team's performance, they are expected to communicate with the sales team about their satisfaction or dissatisfaction. Wherever guidance may be needed, then the owners must provide guidance and support to the sales team.

The reward system established for the sales team must motivate them to improve their performance. If the business offers a sales commission, then the sales commission can be higher once the sales team surpasses its target.

10.5 Increasing sales

While some businesses may meet their sales budget for the year, they must look to increase their sales continuously. If the current market is saturated, then they must look for a new market.

New markets may be sought for the following reasons (ACCA P5 2010):

- An organization might want to extend the product life cycle of a product.

- Where there is intense competition in the home market, an organization might want to escape to less-competitive markets.

- The domestic market offers low growth prospects.

- The domestic market might be risky, and the organization might wish to reduce its exposure to that risk.

With new markets, there may be an increase in the volume and value of sales. If the new markets have fewer competitors, then business owners may be able to charge higher prices in the new market for the same products and services they offered in the existing market.

Once costs are monitored, and there are increases in sales volume and value, then the profit will increase. Most businesses look forward to increasing their profits.

10.6 Evaluating the sales report

After the sales reports are generated, those reports must be evaluated. Sales reports can be evaluated by product, region, by period, etc. Each aspect of the evaluation will help management and the owners to know how they have performed. If their performance was below the target for the period, then they would have to improve. If the sales team's performance surpasses the target, then they must be commended for their great performance.

When the sales reports are evaluated, it provides an opportunity for management to decide where they can improve. The sales report must also be viewed in line with the promotion strategy and budget since promotion helps to increase sales.

11. Increasing promotion

The sales of products and services are expected to increase with increased advertising. Some businesses spend large sums of money to advertise their products and services. When there is an increase in competition, most businesses will often increase their advertising expenditure because their competitors are offering similar or identical products and services.

11.1 Choice of media

When managers and owners are contemplating promoting their products and services, they must evaluate the media options. Each of those media options has its advantages and disadvantages. However, management must choose one or at least a few of them, which will allow them to reach their targeted audience at the most economical cost.

Table 11. Media characteristics

Media	Advantages	Disadvantages
Television	Mass coverage High reach Effect of sight, sound, and motion High prestige Low cost per exposure Attention-getting	Low selectivity Short message life High absolute cost High production costs Clutter

	Strengths	Weaknesses
	Favorable image	
Radio	Local coverage Low cost High frequency Flexibility Low production costs Well-segmented audiences	Audio only Clutter Low attention-getting Fleeting message
Magazines	Segmentation potential Quality reproduction High information content Longevity Multiple readers	Long lead time for ad placement Visual only Lack of flexibility

	Advantages	Disadvantages
Newspapers	High coverage Low cost Short lead time for placing ads Ads can be placed in interest sections Timely (current ads) Reader controls exposure Can be used for coupons	Short life Clutter Low attention-getting capabilities Poor reproduction quality Selective reader exposure
Outdoors	Location-specific High repletion Easily noticed	Short exposure time requires short ads Poor image Local restrictions
Direct mail	High selectivity Reader controls exposure High information content Opportunities for repeat exposure	High cost/contact Poor image (junk email) Clutter

Internet and interactive media	The user selects product information User attention and involvement Interactive relationship Direct selling potential Flexible message platform	Limited creative capabilities Webinar (crowded access) Technology limitations Few valid measurement techniques Limited reach

(Extract from Belch and Belch, 2015)

11.2 Advertising coverage and frequency

As management plans their promotions, they must consider how frequently they want their information to be heard by their audience. Some media choices may have limited coverage, while others will have wider coverage. If management does not have a target audience, then they will have to consider a media choice that provides maximum coverage. Sometimes, maximum coverage can be ineffective since not everyone who hears the promotion has any interest in it. With wider coverage, that option may be very costly.

The media strategies must fit into the sales strategy. Many times, the media strategies will attract those sets of customers that management wants to acquire their goods and services. If the planned media strategies are not effective, then management will have to redesign their media strategies to meet their sales target. During the year, the sales and media strategies must be reviewed. If management and the owners wait until year-end to review their strategies, then they will miss opportunities to improve their performance.

Table 12. Some basic terms and concepts

Terms	Explanation
Media planning	The series of decisions involved in delivering the promotional message to the prospective purchasers and/or users of the product or brand
Media objectives	Specifics
Media strategies	Plan of action designed to attain these objectives
Media	The general category of available delivery systems, including broadcast media, direct marketing, outdoor advertising, and other support media
Media vehicle	The specific carrier within a medium category
Reach	A measure of the number of different audience members exposed at least once to a media vehicle in a given period
Coverage	The potential audience that might receive the message through a media vehicle
Frequency	The number of times the receiver is exposed to the media vehicle in a specific period

(Extract from Belch and Belch, 2015)

11.3 Improving customers' awareness

Customers will sometimes have to hear the same promotion being communicated to them frequently before they decide to utilize the product or service. There is also the need to present the same promotion in different ways.

Some businesses may use the radio and newspaper to promote their goods and services. Other businesses may use the Internet and television to promote their goods and services. The different options used must enhance customers' awareness. Once customers are aware of the goods and services, then management expects those customers to purchase the product and services.

Marketing communications usually consist of several message points that the communicator wants to get across (Belch and Belch 2015).

Figure 17. Stages in customer behavior

(Extract from Cole, 1993)

11.4 Promotion budget

Before management engages in spending for promotion, they ought to establish a promotion budget. The promotion budget is expected to be presented before the fiscal year begins.

The promotion budget must coordinate with the media strategies. In some businesses, the promotion budget may be broken down by products and services. The promotion budget may include figures per month or per quarter. The promotions are expected to provide more awareness to customers, with the intention that they will increase their purchases.

11.5 Marketing promotion mix

Management can use several blends of promotions to get their information to the public. It often requires much effort and skill to attract customers, but everything done is to ensure the business reaches its sales target.

Table 13. Marketing communication mix

Types of promotions	Explanation and examples
Advertising	Any paid form of nonpersonal presentation and promotion of ideas, goods, or services by an identified sponsor via print, broadcast, network, electronic, and display media
Sales promotion	A variety of short-term incentives to encourage the trial or purchase of a product or service, including consumer, trade and business, and sales-force promotions
Events and experiences	Company-sponsored activities and programs designed to create daily or special brand-

	related interactions with consumers, including sports, arts and cause events
Public relations and publicity	A variety of programs directed internally to an employee of the company or externally to consumers, other firms, the government, and the media to promote or protect a company's image or individual products
Direct marketing	The use of email, telephone, fax, or the Internet to communicate directly with or solicit responses or dialogue from specific customers and prospects
Interactive marketing	Online activities and programs designed to engage customers or prospects and directly or indirectly raise awareness, improve the image or elicit sales of products and services
Word of mouth marketing	People-to-people oral, written, or electronic communications relating to the merit of or experiences purchasing or using products or service
Personal selling	Face-to-face interaction with one or more prospective purchasers to make presentations, answering questions, and procuring orders

(Extract from Kotler et al., 2013)

Some small businesses thrive on word-of-mouth marketing. In small communities, it may not be a worthwhile investment to incur much promotional cost to market some products and services, but using word-of-mouth will be the most effective means of conveying the message to those customers.

Directing marketing allows many businesses to increase their sales without incurring many costs. Some large businesses are also involved in direct marketing, as they will send emails to their customers. Repeat customers may be required to complete some forms or submit their email addresses. Once the email address is submitted, sales representatives will constantly send emails to those customers, notifying them of new products and services offered by the business.

Public relations is another way of getting the public informed of the goods and services offered by the organization. Some businesses have monthly information updates where they take great care to keep customers informed of the business's progress and any new goods and services that are available at the business.

12. Establishing competitive selling prices

When business owners start small businesses, they must remember that they will be competing against large and well-established businesses. If those owners want to compete and draw more customers to their businesses, then they must offer competitive selling prices. Most times, customers are willing to purchase from businesses that offer them prices that match their spending power and allow them to save a few dollars.

12.1 Setting prices

It often requires a great deal of work to establish competitive prices. However, once customers find those prices to be competitive and attractive, they will often increase their purchases.

Selecting the pricing objective is critical in setting prices. The managers and owners must establish what they would like to achieve when they set certain prices.

The prices set must make the business competitive. Before setting the price, managers and owners must analyze the prices of their competitors. They must also analyze the cost associated with each good and service.

Figure 18. Setting the price: A chronological description of the price-setting process

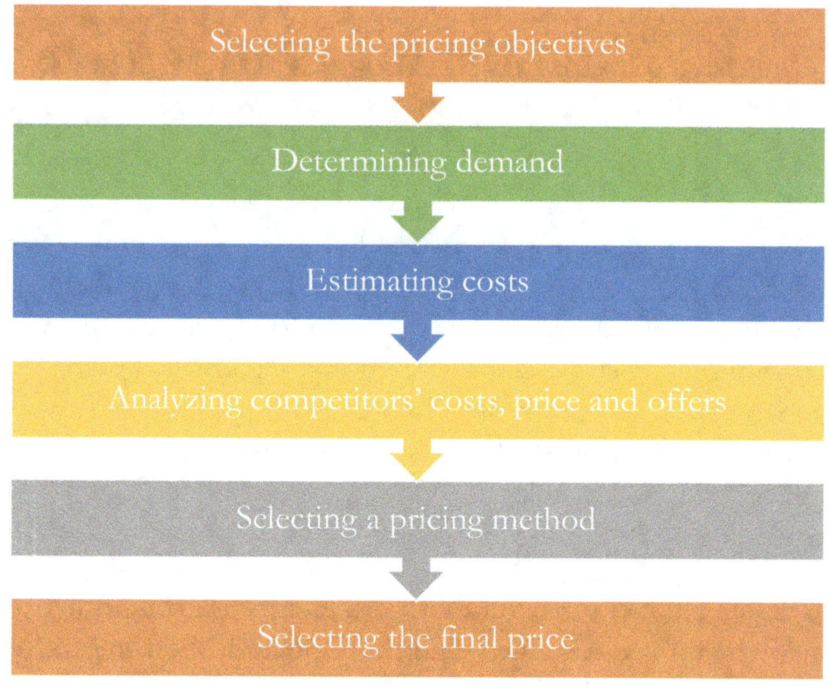

(Extract from Kotler et al., 2013, pp. 518-520)

Demands often vary with prices. When prices are set too high, some customers will seek to purchase goods and services from other suppliers. When prices are low, there is often an increase in purchases. While managers will adjust prices, they must take into consideration the profitability of the organization.

When considering the setting price, managers must perform some analysis of customers' demands. Oftentimes, demands fluctuate with changes in prices.

Whatever prices the business owners and management agree to, the profit made by the business must allow the business to continue its operation. Part of the profits earned can later be used to expand the business.

Some business owners will set their prices after they have identified all possible costs associated with the goods or services they are selling. When there is high competition, some businesses will try to compete with their prices. They may lower their selling prices to attract more customers or reduce the selling prices of a product that is close to its expiration date. However, before they lower their selling prices, they must ensure that all operating and administrative costs are covered.

Table 14. Identifying the cost of production and generating the selling price

Cost/Revenue	Value ($)
A. Direct costs	
Direct materials	12
Direct labor	8
Direct expenses	5
Total direct cost (prime cost)	**25**
B. Overhead	
Direct overhead	5
Total overhead	**5**
Total production cost	**30**
C. Markup	10
D. Selling price	**40**

(Developed by the author for this literature along with extracts from ACCA, CAT, B2 1997)

A slight decrease in the markup may allow some businesses to sell more goods. Some businesses will reduce their selling prices to prevent their inventory from becoming aged inventory.

12.2 Target cost

Some business owners will set target costs. This may be important, especially when there is intense competition.

Target cost is an estimate of a product cost that is derived by subtracting the desired profit from the competitive market price (ACCA P5 2010).

With a target cost, managers need to work along with their team to match their production and operation costs to meet the target cost set. That approach often forces managers and their supporting employees to be efficient in their operations. They will have to eliminate waste. They are sometimes forced to utilize their resources more productively.

Table 15. Target cost computation for a typical organization

Components to target cost	Value ($)
Competitor's selling price	25
Less the desired profit (the organization seeks)	(5)
Target cost (to be delivered by the organization)	20

In the example provided in Table 15, the selling prices are set at $25. The owners need a profit of $5. Therefore, the managers and their teams must ensure that operation and production costs do not surpass $20. With a target cost, business owners can ensure that their goods and services are competitive in the market.

12.3 Lowering costs

Every manager and owner must seek to lower the cost of their operation. It is not an impossible thing for them to do. They must reconsider their operation and seek cost-efficient ways.

When costs are lower, then businesses can be competitive. Their ability to compete effectively may result in them increasing their overall profits and also expanding their businesses.

13. Carefully managing costs

Managing costs can be difficult, but it is not impossible. Those who are responsible for managing the business must manage the cost of the business. If they allow the costs to be high, then it will erode their profits, and soon they will be out of business.

13.1 Measures to control costs

The business cannot remain competitive if prices constantly increase. There are times when costs must be managed so that customers pay less but get more in return.

Figure 19. Measures to control business costs

13.1.1 Set objectives to reduce costs and evaluate those objectives

If management wants to reduce costs, then they must set some objectives. When objectives are set, managers will be strategic in their operations.

Reducing costs must be something of which all employees are aware. Each employee must know how their activity will impact the overall cost to the organization. When employees take responsibility for their actions by buying into cost reduction, it can help management to achieve their objectives to reduce costs while maximizing profit.

13.1.2 Recruit competent individuals

Recruiting specialists to operate in some areas may help to reduce costs compared to employing non-specialists. Oftentimes, specialists will deliver quality output with little waste of time and probably no waste of resources.

The cost for one specialist will be higher than the cost for an employee who provides general service at the same level. However, when specialists are recruited, they reduce waste and will produce more than the generalist. Many times, specialists identify problems and provide solutions. Once specialists are given the scope to perform their duties, their benefits will often outweigh their employment costs.

13.1.3 Establishing long-term relationships with suppliers

When suppliers know that they have long-term relationships with customers, they may be more flexible with the prices they charge customers. Some long-term suppliers may provide discounts to their customers since they are aware that they will recover any discount offered to customers.

Many suppliers want to be assured that they have a market to sell their goods and services. Therefore, suppliers will be delighted to reward long-term customers for the assurance that they will continue to acquire goods and services from them.

13.1.4 Purchasing large quantities

Customers who often purchase large quantities are often entitled to reduced costs. For example, suppliers may waive some logistic costs for those customers who purchase large quantities of goods.

With large-scale purchases, customers may be entitled to volume discounts. Suppliers may offer higher discounts for those customers who purchase large quantities.

13.1.5 Acquiring quality inputs

When quality inputs are acquired, it reduces waste and rework. When there is a demand for rework, then costs will increase. Materials that do not meet the business's expectation can result in customers rejecting the final product.

The procurement policy must speak to the issue of acquiring quality inputs. Yes, quality inputs will cost more than poor-quality inputs, but overall, quality inputs reduce the overall cost of the business.

13.1.6 Reducing the need to purchase from middlemen

Every time goods pass through middlemen, there will be additional costs since those middlemen have to make profits. So, managers must purchase directly from suppliers to reduce input costs. To purchase from some suppliers, customers may have to purchase larger quantities. That may be possible if they plan their purchases and reduce regular purchases of smaller quantities.

13.1.7 Eliminate non-value-added activities

Wherever there are non-value-added activities, those activities must be removed. Managers will have to constantly evaluate the business for areas where non-value-added activities exist.

There may be the need to merge some activities, so instead of doing one thing at a time, several things may be done simultaneously. With the merging of activities, operational costs will be reduced.

Sometimes, there may not be the need to have many employees execute some activities.

13.1.8 Great use of advanced technology

If businesses are not utilizing advanced technology, they need to invest in it. If the business is using outdated machinery and equipment, then it may be time to have modern machinery and equipment. Many times, older machinery and equipment are expensive to maintain. Advanced technology will often reduce costs and produce better output.

13.1.9 Benchmark costs against industry standard

Business owners must benchmark their costs against other businesses in the same industry. The reason why some businesses are not competitive with their selling price is because their cost is above the industry average.

Once business owners evaluate their costs against the industry average, then they will have to take action. One such action may be to reduce their costs, to make their goods and services competitive.

13.1.10 Providing a reward for cost reduction

Employees like to be rewarded for their contributions. If the owners want to reduce costs and they engage the employees, they can also choose to reward employees for participating in reducing the business cost. Many times, employees know of areas where costs must be reduced. The reward to those who assist in reducing costs will motivate them to assist the business in reaching its cost-reduction objectives.

13.1.11 Regular maintenance of machinery and equipment

If machinery and equipment are not maintained regularly, then their operating costs, in the long run, will be high. Some managers will embrace preventative maintenance. With frequent and timely maintenance, defects will be identified and addressed before they worsen. When parts have to be replaced because of poor maintenance, it may happen at a time when the business has great demands from customers. To replace some parts suddenly can be very expensive since some parts may have to be sourced from overseas. Because of the urgent need to import some parts, then airfreight will be incurred instead of sea freight. Airfreight is always more expensive, but the downtime is less.

13.1.12 Reducing the use of paper in the business

Several business owners have reduced the use of paper. Most of their documentation is stored in their database. Instead of printing some documents, employees will carefully store those documents in the database.

Some businesses have moved away from paying employees via cheque. They will transfer employees' compensation directly to their bank accounts. Pay slips for employees are sent to the employees' email addresses.

Reducing paper can be one less cost to deal with. Whenever documents are printed, then storage space has to be allocated to store those printed documents. Some businesses send the board of directors packages to the director electronically, which reduces the need to print documents for board meetings.

14. Acquiring and storing inventory

Businesses that have to produce goods and services will have to acquire some amount of inventory. They will use the goods they acquired in their production to produce the outcome that customers need. Other businesses acquired goods and sell the goods on without any modification.

Acquiring groceries for domestic use is different from acquiring inventory for the business. Therefore, business owners and managers will have to follow procurement policy.

14.1 Procurement policy

When many businesses have just started, they may operate without any procurement policy. However, after some months or years, the owners may request that a procurement policy be established. Many times, if the owners are not involved in the day-to-day operations of the business, then they have to rely on the managers and other employees to do the correct things.

Inventory is one area where some businesses experience much pilfering. There must be an adequate safeguard to detect and prevent inventory thieves.

It may take some time to develop a procurement policy, but it is important to have one. In the absence of a procurement policy, employees may do things that are not beneficial to the business. When designing a procurement policy, some important components must be included in it. For some businesses, their procurement policy may include many areas to guide employees about procurement. For other businesses, their procurement policies may be brief but still cover some essential areas.

Figure 20. Components of a procurement policy

- Name of the organization
- Date when the policy was submitted or approved
- Table of contents
- Introduction and procurement objectives
- Glossary, terminologies, definitions
- Methods of procurement
- Characteristics of goods, services, constructions, ideas
- Medium for advertising tenders
- Duration for advertising tenders
- Opening, accepting, and rejecting tenders
- Restricted and single-source tendering
- Evaluation requirements and templates
- Composition of evaluation committee
- How and when to award contracts
- Approval levels for contract sums
- Ethics for procurement
- Confidentiality and disclosure statement

When managers are designing the procurement policy, they must include written information for each of the main components that they include in the policy. The written information must be simple enough to guide a user of the policy to make consistent decisions for the benefit of the business.

When new procurement policies are established for small businesses, there must be training for employees to understand certain procurement terms. Even if they have had general training, there will be a need for refresher training, especially if employees are not following the guidelines stated in the procurement policy. Training will be needed for any new employees who will have to be involved in procurement.

14.2 The Procurement and Inventory Departments

Many businesses have Procurement and Inventory Departments. Those two departments have their separate duties to perform. However, they both depend on each other. Before inventory can be acquired, the inventory Department will have to provide updates on their inventory balances.

For large businesses, department heads may send their purchase requests to the Procurement Department. The Procurement Department will assess the purchase request (PR) and then generate the purchase order (PO). When the inventory is received, it will be stored in the warehouse. Small businesses may not have large warehouses, or they may revert to storing inventory within the store. When inventory is received, the warehouse or inventory employees will verify the actual goods received against the delivery note and will also compare the actual inventory received against the purchase order.

14.3 Acquiring inventory

Before acquiring inventory, certain requirements must be met. There must be a need for the inventory. The required forms must be completed and then submitted for approval. Oftentimes, managers will purchase from established suppliers since they can rely on the quality of the goods they will receive.

Most times, when managers are placing orders to acquire goods, they will purchase from suppliers who will grant them discounts and a longer duration to settle the outstanding balance. When suppliers and customers enjoy a good relationship, some costs may be waived since those suppliers expect their customers to be repeat customers.

The quantities of inventory acquired must allow the business to meet the needs of its customers. To avoid making frequent purchases, some small businesses will acquire large quantities of inventory at once.

When acquiring inventories for small businesses, some managers will use the Just in Time (JIT) purchasing approach since they want to minimize the inventory they have on hand. With the use of JIT purchasing, managers will reduce the amount of cash tied up on holding inventory since the inventory is purchased just before the customer needs it or just before it goes into production.

Table 16. Essential elements of JIT

Element	Detail
JIT Purchasing	Parts and raw materials should be purchased as near as possible to the time they are needed, using frequent small deliveries against bulk contracts. Inventory levels are therefore minimized.
Close relationship with suppliers	In a JIT environment, the responsibility for the quality of goods lies with the supplier. A long-term commitment between supplier and customer should therefore be established. If an organization has confidence that suppliers will deliver material of 100% quality, on time, so that there will be no rejects or returns and hence no consequent production delays, usage of materials can be matched with the delivery of materials, and inventories can be kept at near-zero levels.

Uniform loading	All parts of the production process should be operated at a speed that matches the rate at which the final product is demanded by the customer. Production runs will therefore be shorter, and there will be smaller inventories of finished goods because the output is being matched more closely to demand (and so storage costs will be reduced).
Set-up time reduction	Machinery set-ups are non-value-added activities that should be reduced or even eliminated.
Machine cells	Machines or workers should be grouped by product or component instead of by the type of work performed. Products can flow from a machine without having to wait for the next stage of processing or returning to stores. Lead times and work in progress are thus reduced.
Quality	Production management should seek to eliminate scrap and defective units during production and avoid the need for a reworking of units since this delays production and leads to late deliveries to customers. Product quality and production quality are important "drivers" in a JIT system.
Pull system (Kanban)	Products/components are only produced when needed by the next process. Nothing is produced in anticipation of need, to then remain in inventory, consuming resources.

Preventive maintenance	The production system must be reliable and prompt without unforeseen delays and breakdowns.
Employee involvement	Workers within each machine cell should be trained to operate each machine within that cell and to be able to perform routine preventative maintenance on the cell machines (i.e. to be multiskilled and flexible).

(Extracted from ACCA P5, 2010, pp. 396-397)

When acquiring inventory, managers must assess the warehouse space to determine if they have enough space to store the quantity of inventory they will purchase. In cases where large quantities have to be purchased, and there is not enough space currently available, then arrangements must be made to rent additional temporary warehouse space. Some small businesses will increase their purchases of inventories beyond their current warehouse capacity because they forecast shortages or predict that there will be a sudden great demand for the goods.

Managers must forecast their inventory needs. They must also create a cash flow forecast to determine the amount of cash outflow that will be used to acquire the inventory.

14.4 Storing inventory

The inventory storage place must have adequate lighting. Some inventories must be stored at cool or hot temperatures, so special arrangements must be in place to keep them at that specific temperature.

Inventories will be damaged if they are stored poorly. Small businesses cannot afford to write off large volumes of damaged inventory since it will affect the continuity of the business.

The place where the inventory is stored must allow customers to easily collect their items. Most times, when customers make their purchases, they need to have their items immediately.

15. Purchasing on credit

Small business owners must establish good relationships with suppliers. They must also seek to establish credit agreements with suppliers since that will be one way of reducing their demands to find the cash to purchase inventory immediately.

Credit purchases must be made with strict guidelines. Only authorized employees of the business must engage in credit purchases on behalf of the business.

While it may be easy to access credit purchases, there must be controls in place. Credit purchases must be evaluated against the business's ability to pay in a timely manner, according to the credit terms. Also, management must perceive that there will be a demand for the goods by customers.

If some suppliers offer credit, they may not offer a discount to the same customers. Therefore, customers must determine if they are willing to sacrifice the discount compared to the credit they will receive.

Managers must seek to establish legal agreements with suppliers. The legal agreement will formalize each party's legal obligations, and in the event they have problems, they can take legal action.

Suppliers may only offer credit to customers who are engaged in long-term purchases. Credit may also be offered to customers who purchase large quantities. Therefore, if managers want to benefit from credit, they may have to meet those two requirements. With constant large volume purchases, suppliers will evaluate each customer, and once they determine that those customers are reliable, a credit facility can be offered.

When credit is offered, managers must schedule payments to suppliers. Some managers will use Accounts Payable to determine their next payments to suppliers. All suppliers will not be paid at the same time since their payment periods will be different. Although some suppliers' balances may be due for longer periods, managers must allocate enough cash to make those future payments.

Managers can capitalize on credit purchases since they will have immediate access to the goods they need. If they were to wait until they have enough cash to make their purchases, they might eventually lose sales. Losing one-day sales will have an impact on the organization's profit and cash flow.

Some goods are sold in large quantities during certain seasons. Therefore, managers must ensure that they have the goods that customers need. The managers must purchase those goods in advance, as they wait for customers to purchase large quantities during certain seasons. Anticipating customers' demands will aid in determining possible credit purchases to meet future demands.

16. Credit sales to customers

Sometimes, to generate more sales, managers must consider the option of offering credit to customers. It is always risky to sell goods to customers on credit, but it may be a great opportunity to enhance the organization's sales. When credit is offered to customers they may increase their purchases, since they have the opportunity to benefit from the goods right away and then pay later.

16.1 Risk preference

If the owners do not have a large appetite for risk, then they may not consider credit sales. The owners will be comfortable with selling goods and receiving cash immediately. Some business owners think that it is too much work to monitor credit customers. However, in some businesses, the sales from credit customers outweigh their cash customers.

Business owners may choose to charge higher selling prices to credit customers. The higher price is intended to allow the business to benefit from the absence of immediate cash.

Business owners who think credit sales will increase their profits may agree to offer credit to customers. Those owners may be risk seekers and want to enhance the overall profitability of their business.

Table 17. Risk Preference

Risk preference	Explanation
Risk-averse	A decision-maker who acts on the assumption that the worst outcome might occur
Risk neutral	A decision-maker who is concerned with what will be the most likely outcome
Risk seeker	A decision-maker who is interested in the best outcome no matter how small the chance that it may occur

(Extracted from ACCA P5, 2010)

16.2 Credit duration

Those businesses that will be offering credit must determine the credit duration. With a longer credit duration, there is a great likelihood that customers may not settle their balances.

When some businesses start, the owners oftentimes will only sell goods for cash. However, as business owners become more aware of the market, they may consider offering credit for short durations. Once it is proven that customers settle their outstanding balances in a timely manner, then business owners may offer longer credit durations.

In some businesses, a longer credit duration will be offered at a higher interest rate to credit customers. In others, credit will be offered at one standard interest rate since the owners will be earning greater interest income from a longer credit duration.

Once business owners want to offer credit for a longer duration, they will need to establish a credit or collection department. This department will be tasked with following up with customers who have outstanding balances and have them settle those balances promptly.

16.3 Credit criteria for customers

Before offering credit to customers, business owners, along with their managers, must determine the criteria for offering credit to customers. Once the criteria for credit are established then such information must be shared with the credit and sales employees.

The criteria established must be good enough to attract customers but, at the same time, deter customers who look like they will be unable to settle their outstanding balances. Managers must be strict at enforcing the credit criteria since they will be accountable for any bad debt that has to be written off.

16.4 Managing accounts receivable reports

Managing the accounts receivable report is something that managers must do regularly. The accounts receivable reports will have to be presented to the business owners. Greater efforts must be made to prevent customers from settling their installments beyond the agreed period. Once customers start missing some installments, they might eventually be unable to settle their full outstanding balances. Follow-up calls to customers are very important. Customers ought to be contacted before their due date, just as a reminder for them to pay their installment on time.

17. Managing cash inflows and outflows

Without money flowing into the business, many businesses will fail. Some people with great ideas are unable to start their businesses because they do not have the capital, while some businesses fail because their finances were not properly managed.

The lack of finance in the business can result in managers not being able to capitalize on discounts for cash purchases. Some suppliers only sell their goods for cash; therefore, when managers have to purchase goods from those suppliers, they must be ready to pay immediately.

17.1 Inflows

Every business would like to increase its cash inflows. Customers can pay them directly with cash or through the bank. More and more businesses are encouraging customers to pay them through direct bank payments. Direct bank transfers eliminate the problem of customers presenting counterfeit notes. Employees in small businesses may not always have currency counters with the technology to detect counterfeit notes. Many of the people who create counterfeit notes have increased their skills in creating such illegal notes to the point where it is difficult to detect such notes with the human eye.

Sometimes, when customers have to pay in cash, they may engage in small-value purchases. However, if they are allowed to make purchases via direct bank payment, then they may buy more goods.

Managers must manage the inflows. They must drive more inflows. They will have to increase sales and also encourage credit customers to settle their balance on or before the due date.

It is through the inflows that businesses will have enough funds to settle outflows. Many times, the inflows and outflows will not match, but every effort must be made to have enough inflows to meet the demands of the outflows. Inflows can include sales of goods, payment for services, or repayment by credit customers. Some businesses may have a treasury officer or treasury manager. The individual who occupies this position will have to increase the inflow of funds.

17.2 Outflows

Many managers like to have inflows of funds, but they are not always delighted with the outflows. Having outflows is not bad, but those outflows must be carefully managed.

The treasury officer or treasury manager must carefully plan the outflows of funds. They may have to straddle some outflows based on the funds they have in the business. Whenever managers are approaching a deadline to make some payments, and they do not have enough funds in the business to meet those outflows, they may have to consider selling some goods at discounted prices. Sometimes, it may be difficult to access a loan to manage the business in the short term. Therefore, selling some goods at discounted prices will allow enough funds to be available for urgent outflows. Some outflows that businesses will be engaged in are payments to suppliers, paying utility bills, payment of wages and salaries, etc.

17.3 Projects and capital expenditures

Some businesses may be engaged in major projects and capital expenditures, especially if they want to expand their operation. At the start of a business, the business owners may be delighted to operate at a small scale because they were uncertain of the market. However, after being involved in business for some years, they may choose to expand the business to meet the needs of customers.

With business expansion, there will first be cash outflows. The cash outflows can last for several months or years. However, it is expected that there will be greater cash inflows over time, thus allowing the business to have enough funds.

Major projects and capital expenditures must be carefully evaluated. The project must provide evidence that it will be economically viable. Every owner likes to know that they have enough funds at hand. Owners often look at ways to grow their cash at hand and bank balances.

18. Security for the business

With security arrangements put in place, the assets of the business will be protected. If the owners and managers fail to provide security for the business, all of their success can easily be eroded. Business owners invest too much to leave their assets exposed to persons who are interested in taking their gains. Some people plan to steal the assets of the organization. Employees are among some of the people who often steal from their employers.

18.1 Physical security

One way of protecting the business's assets is through physical security. This will include security guards, locks on doors, and dual custody of certain sensitive areas of the business. Although businesses may have locks on their doors, they may still choose to employ guards. It is better to have more security guards than to have fewer security guards. When certain assets are lost, no amount of compensation can restore them.

18.2 Surveillance

Business owners may also choose to install surveillance. This security arrangement will allow the owners to review any illegal activities that occur when the physical security fails to detect any wrongdoings.

If there is collusion among employees, it is often difficult for business owners to identify illegal activities. However, with the support of surveillance, business owners will be able to review a video to see what transpired. With surveillance, employees will be able to detect people who may be attempting to commit illegal activities against the business.

18.3 Data protection

When businesses have integrated information systems, they must protect their data. Hackers often try to invade the business's database. If some data is lost, it can harm the business's image or prevent the business from operating.

Constantly, a business must protect its data. It will have to upgrade its data protection periodically, as hackers and viruses are constantly trying to invade its databases.

Reference list

ACCA 2.1. (2000). *Information Systems*. London: Foulks Lynch.

ACCA 2.4. (2001). *Financial management and control*. London: Foulks Lynch.

ACCA 3.4. (2003). *Business Information Management*. London: Foulks Lynch.

ACCA P5. (2010). *Advanced performance management*. BPP House.

Belch, G E., & Belch, M. A. *Advertising and Promotion: An Integrated Marketing Communications Perspective*, 10th ed. New York: McGraw-Hill, 2015.

Cole, G. A. (1993). *Management theory and practice*, 4th ed. ELBS with DP Publication.

Hughes, R., Ginnett, R., & Curphy, G. (2015). *Leadership: Enhancing the Lessons of Experience*. 8th ed. New York: McGraw-Hill Education.

Kotler, P., Keller, K.L., Ang, S. H., Leong, S, W., & Tan, C-T. (2013). *Marketing Management: An Asian Perspective*, 6th ed. Singapore: Pearson Education South Asia Pte Ltd.

Lane, P. (1966). *Revision Notes for Ordinary Level Economics*. London: Allman & Son Limited.

Noe, R. A., Hollenbeck, J.R., Gerhart, B., & Wright, P. M. (2015). *Human Resource Management: Gaining a Competitive Advantage*. 9th ed. New York: McGraw-Hill Education.

Thompson, A., Peteraf, M., Gamble, J., & Strickland, A. J. III. (2014). *Crafting and Executing Strategy: The Quest for Competitive Advantage: Concepts and Cases*. 19th ed. New York: McGraw-Hill Education.

Titman, S., Martin, T., Keown, A. J., & Martin, J. D. (2016). *Financial Management: Principles and Applications*. 7th ed. Pearson Australia.

About the author

Having a heart for small business owners, author Geary Reid penned his thoughts to help them know what they have to do to start a small business and how they will make their business successful. Not everyone will be able to establish a large business, but many people will start with small businesses, and then they will grow their businesses.

The requirements for small businesses are many, and while many people have started small businesses, their businesses have not been able to grow continuously. However, Chartered Accountant Geary Reid provides many hands-on approaches for growth. As business owners apply his essential information, their businesses will expand. The growth must not be a one-off event but continuous.

Many small business owners have great ideas but lack technical knowledge about different aspects of the business. They sometimes need additional financing for their business, but they do not know how to approach the issue of obtaining it.

As small businesses grow, the owners need to recruit competent persons to help them manage their businesses. Both recently recruited employees and those who have been working for many years with the business will need training. Once those employees are trained and know what has to be done, then business owners must delegate some authority to them, as the business owners will then have more time to analyze the entire operation. Knowing that many small business owners are afraid to delegate or do not know how to delegate authority effectively, author Geary Reid has provided careful guidance on how business owners can be effective in delegating authority to their employees.

Business owners must invest in integrated information systems to carefully monitor their businesses. While business owners do not have to direct the daily operations of the business, they can analyze the performance of the business and their employees and make critical decisions. Once the integrated information system is effectively implemented and used, then it provides a quick and wide overview of the entire business.

The owner and managers must carefully manage the cash flow. Geary Reid provides many useful guides on how to increase sales and increase customers' awareness of the goods and services. He expects owners and managers will manage the cost of the business so that there is enough money to pay suppliers, pay employees, and have some money left over for future investments.

Operating small businesses will no longer be a difficult thing for many small business owners, as they now have practical information to guide their decisions. They can grow their small businesses into large-scale operations because they are better equipped with the information provided by their new and concerned friend, Geary Reid.